THE TOW NGOLLEN

AN ARTISTIC IMPRESSION

OF AN AREA OF

OUTSTANDING BEAUTY & INTEREST

SURROUNDING

THE ANCIENT TOWN & VALE OF LLANGOLLEN

DAVID S.YERBURGH

2005

PREFACE

The attraction of North Wales, by its romantic scenery, the antiquity of its language, and the well authenticated records of its desperate struggle for its independence, renders every part of the Principality interesting, and perhaps none more so than the beautifully picturesque and interesting neighbourhood of Llangollen, which has deservedly excited the attention and admiration of strangers and antiquarians. Nor have the expectations of its numerous visitors been disappointed; for, though the Alps may raise their towering summits to a greater height – may embosum in their dark recesses more ample lakes, and give rise to more magnificent rivers – yet even they cannot present a more pleasing variety of scenery, or more picturesque views, than those with which Llangollen is surrounded.'

These words provided part of the introduction to Simpson's account of '*The Town and Vale of Llangollen'*, a small leather bound book written in 1837. As such, they also act as an ideal preface to this present book, which attempts to recapture something of the splendour and variety of the scenery that surrounds the town and Vale of Llangollen in the twenty-first century and to illustrate this with various engravings, drawings and photographs.

David S.Yerburgh

****

ISBN 0 9535 6355 3

Published by
Revd. Canon David Yerburgh,
2, Mill Race Close, Mill Road, Salisbury,
Wiltshire. SP2 7RX

INTRODUCTION

In the spring of 2004 and in the summer of 2005 I spent a very rewarding two weeks in a delightful cottage on the outskirts of Llangollen, which became the base for these tours of Llangollen and its surrounding area. For the purpose of this small book I have divided these tours into six different areas, all of which could well be subdivided into different individual tours.

Tour one is of the town of Llangollen itself and includes the Llangollen Canal and Railway, Castell Dinas Bran and the famous Trevor and Eglwyseg rocks opposite it.

Tour two covers the area north west of Llangollen to Rhuddlan Castle via Valle Crucis Abbey, the Horseshoe Pass, some delightful village churches, St Asaph Cathedral and the towns of Ruthin and Denbigh.

Tour three takes in the area north east of Llangollen and includes, three superb town churches, two castles built by the Welsh Princes and two built by the English, a healing well and the ruins of an abbey. This tour also includes the former industrial Clywedog Valley, which concludes with a visit to Erddig House and Gardens.

Tour four is the area south east of Llangollen, which includes the two National Trust Castles of Chirk and Powis and the two Border castles at Dolforwyn (Welsh) and Montgomery (English), both having been renovated by CADW.

Tour five covers the area south west of Llangollen and really could be an area by itself. This includes three beautiful valleys. The first is the charming former industrial valley of Afon Ceiriog. The second is the valley of Afon Rhaeadr and leads to the highest waterfall in Wales. The third is the valley of Afon Tanat, which leads to the pilgrim's church at Pennant Melangell.

The final tour is the area west of Llangollen and more or less follows Thomas Telford's amazing road as far as the waterfall at Pont y Glyn, via the ancestral home of Owain Glyndwr and two charming small churches now in the care of CADW.

Taken together these six tours give a real taste of the beauty and the history of the town and the countryside in and around Llangollen. My hope is that anyone who follows some of these tours will also get an insight into the stunning scenery of this area and a better understanding of it ancient heritage.

Most people who visit Wales today will soon come across a simple anonymous nineteenth century rhyme entitled '*Seven Wonders of Wales'*, which runs as follows:-

Pistyll Rhaeadr and Wrexham Steeple
Snowdon's Mountain without its people,
Overton Yew Trees, St Winefride's Well,
Langollen Bridge and Gresford Bells.

This simple rhyme was obviously written by someone who came from the north east part of Wales as six of the seven 'wonders' are to be found in the area covered by this small book! Even the seventh, 'Snowdon's Mountain' is visible on a clear day from the top of the Horseshoe Pass.

This book of tours will, I hope, show that the Wonders of Wales are not limited to seven, but are almost unlimited; for its churches, castles, stately homes, mountains and valleys are legion and are all worthy of being included as 'The Wonders of Wales'.

David S.Yerburgh
Salisbury
2005

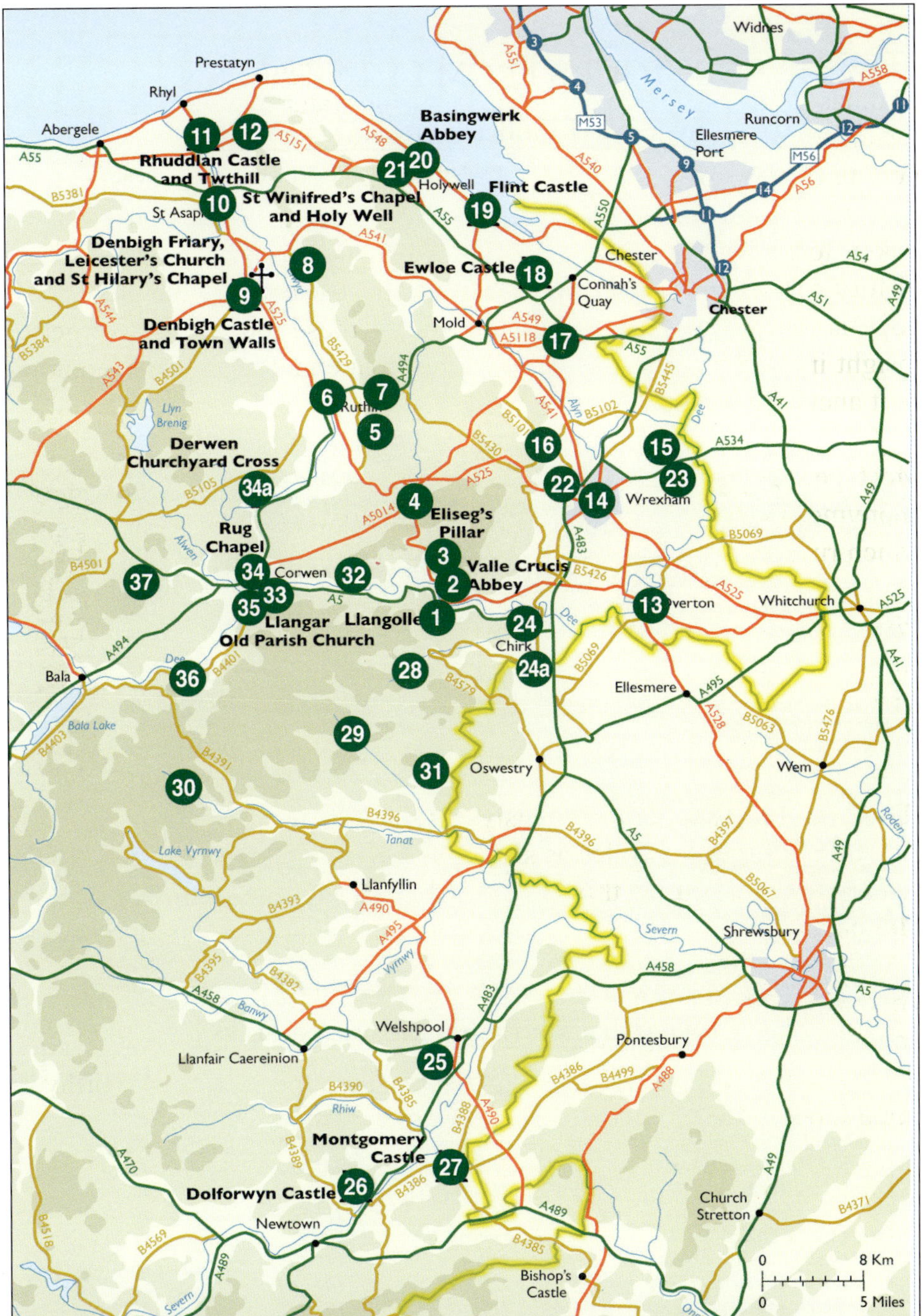

Reproduced by kind permission of Cadw. Crown Copyright.

SIX TOURS FROM LLANGOLLEN

TOUR ONE LLANGOLLEN TOWN & SURROUNDS

Map No. Place	Explorer Map	Reference	Page
1. St Collen's Church, Llangollen	*256*	*216 420*	*11*
1. Plas Newydd, Llangollen	*256*	*219 417*	*13*
1. Llangollen Bridge & River Dee	*256*	*215 422*	*15*
1. Llangollen Canal from ***Horseshoe Falls***	*256*	*196 433*	
to Llangollen Wharf	*256*	*215 424*	*17*
1. Llangollen Canal from Llangollen Wharf			
to Pontcysyllte Aqueduct	*256*	*270 421*	*19*
24. Pontcysyllte Aqueduct			
24. to Chirk Aqueduct	*256*	*279 372*	*19*
1. The Railway from Llangollen to ***Carrog***	*256*	*118.435*	*21*
1. Castell Dinas Bran	*256*	*224 431*	*23*
1. Offa's Dyke Path from Trevor Rocks	*256*	*227 435*	*25*
to Eglwyseg Rocks	*256*	*217 450*	*25*
to World's End	*256*	*235 478*	*25*

TOUR TWO, NORTH WEST FROM LLANGOLLEN

2. Valle Crucis Abbey	*256*	*207 441*	*28*
3. Eliseg's Pillar	*256*	*203 446*	*28*
4. The Horseshoe Pass	*256*	*186 471*	*29*
5.Castell Rhodwdd	*256*	*177 516*	*29*
5. Llanarmon-yn lal	*256*	*193 563*	*29*
5. Llanfair Dyffryn Clwyd	*256*	*133 555*	*29*
6. Ruthin Church	*256*	*125 585*	*33*
6. Ruthin Castle	*256*	*123 581*	*33*
7. St Dyfnog's Church, Llanrhaeadr	*265*	*082 635*	*34*
8. St Marcella's Church, Egwys-Wen	*265*	*071 662*	*34*
9. Denbigh Castle	*265*	*054 657*	*35*
9. Lord Leicester's Church	*265*	*054 657*	*35*
9. Denbigh Friary	*265*	*060 667*	*35*
10. St Asaph's Cathedral	*264*	*037 743*	*39*
11. Rhuddlan Castle	*264*	*025 778*	*41*
11. Twthill,Motte & Bailey	*264*	*027 777*	*41*
12. Dyserth Waterfall and Church	*265*	*057 798*	*43*

TOUR THREE, NORTH EAST FROM LLANGOLLEN

Map No. Reference	Place Page		Landrnger Map
13. Overton Parish Church	*117*	*373 418*	*47*
14. Wrexham Parish Church	*117*	*335 505*	*47*
15. Gresford Parish Churches	*117*	*347 550*	*47*
16. Caergwrle (Welsh Castle)	*117*	*306 573*	*49*
17. Hawarden (English Castle)	*117*	*316 655*	*49*
18. Ewloe Castle (Welsh Castle)	*117*	*288 675*	*51*
19. Flint Castle (English Castle)	*117*	*248 735*	*51*
20. Holywell, St Winefride's Well	*116*	*184 764*	*53*
21. Basingwerk Abbey	*116*	*195 775*	*53*

SIX TOURS FROM LLANGOLLEN, CONTINUED

TOUR THREE CONTINUED THE CLYWEDOG VALLEY

TOUR FOUR, SOUTH EAST FROM LLANGOLLEN

TOUR FIVE, SOUTH WEST FROM LLANGOLLEN, THE CEIRIOG VALLEY

TOUR SIX, WEST FROM LLANGOLLEN

TOUR ONE
LLANGOLLEN TOWN & SURROUNDS

St Collen's Parish Church

Plas Newydd

The Medieval Town Bridge & Walks by the River Dee

The Horseshoe Falls to Llangollen Canal Wharf

The Llangollen Canal Wharf to Chirk Aqueduct

Llangollen Station & Railway to Carrog

Castell Dinas Bran

Offa's Dyke Path from Panorama Walk to World's End

The Grotto & Font at Plas Newydd

Photograph by Diana Coleridge

2004

St Collen's, Church, Llangollen

Black & White Steel Engraving

Engraved by C.Mottram

From an Original Drawing by H. Gastineau

1831

START OF TOUR ONE

LLANGOLLEN & SURROUNDS

The Parish Church of St Collen

The obvious place to start a tour of the town of Llangollen is **the medieval church of St Collen**. Llan is the Welsh for church or enclosure and Collen was a seventh century saint who chose this place to build his hermitage. The combination of the two words, Llan and Collen, go to make up the present day name of the town of Llangollen.

The church, as one sees it today, remains much as it was after the major restoration of 1863, when the present chancel, south aisle and door into the tower were added to the original medieval church. The exact date of this original medieval church is uncertain, except that it replaced an earlier wooden structure established by St Collen.

The outstanding glory of Llangollen Parish Church is the two superbly carved 15th century oak hammer-beam roofs. The most elaborately carved section of the centre roof is now at the east-end of the nave, where originally it would have acted as a '*Canopy of Honour*' over the high altar.

In the churchyard, near the main entrance to the church, can be seen the distinctive triangular tomb marking the burial place of *the 'Ladies of Llangollen'* and their devoted housekeeper Mary Carryl. They lived just above the church at **Plas Newydd**, which makes a good place to visit after seeing the Church of St Collen.

Plas Newydd, near Llangollen

The Seat of the Late Lady Eleanor Butler and Miss Ponsonby

Drawn on Stone by W.L.Walton

From a Picture by Edwin W. Jacques

c. 1829

TOUR ONE CONTINUED

LLANGOLLEN & SURROUNDS

Plas Newydd, the home of 'The Ladies of Llangollen'

In 1778 Lady Eleanor Butler and Miss Sarah Ponsonby eloped from their two families in Ireland and came to Wales. In 1780 they set up their home at Pen-y-Maes cottage in Llangollen, which they renamed as **Plas Newydd (New Hall).** They lived together at Plas Newydd for nearly fifty years until the death of Lady Eleanor Butler in 1829.

While at Plas Newydd they spent much of their time in writing, reading, sketching and embroidering, as well as re-designing the gardens all of which earned them the title '*The Ladies of Llangollen*'.

Between 1778 and 1780 '*The Ladies*' began a programme of elaborate 'gothicisation' of the house, which included the insertion of oriel windows with stained glass and a mass of collected carved oak panels, often the gifts of friends.

The Elizabethan style of black battens on the front of the present house were the work of General Yorke, who bought the house in 1876. He was also responsible for much of the wooden carving on the outside of the house.

The picturesque garden, which '*The Ladies*' created, with its romantic vistas, gravel paths, rustic seats, viewing points, summerhouse and bowers soon became neglected and overgrown. However recently, thanks to a lottery grant, the garden is being restored to its former glory.

Both the house and the garden are open to the public.

Llangollen Bridge & Castell Dinas Bran

Black and White Etching by W.Batenham

19th century

TOUR ONE CONTINUED

LLANGOLLEN & SURROUNDS

The Medieval Bridge over the River Dee & Riverside Walks

Practically every one who visits the centre of the busy town of Llangollen will have to cross **the fine stone four arched bridge over the River Dee** considered to be one of *'The Seven Wonders of Wales'*. This splendid bridge was first built in 1345 by John Trevor I, the Bishop of St Asaph, and who had a local home at Trevor Hall on the outskirts of Llangollen.

When John Trevor I built this bridge it was the only stone bridge across the Dee for very many miles and before that time people had to cross the Dee by boat.

Llangollen Bridge was rebuilt in the seventeenth century. This particular structure remained the same on the lower side and was perfectly copied on the upper side when it was widened in 1873 and again in 1969. When the railway came to Llangollen the actual road over the bridge had to be raised in order to provide a further square arch over the new railway, which rather spoilt the perfect symmetry of the original bridge.

On the railway side of the town there is a very pleasant walk along the canal path, which follows the River Dee all the way to Horseshoe Falls. On the other side of the river there is a charming short riverside walk, from which one can get the best views of Llangollen Bridge and the turbulent River Dee as it flows rapidly under the bridge.

Llantisilio Church

Black & White Steel Engraving

Engraved by H.Adlard

From an Original Drawing by H.Gastineau

1831

TOUR ONE CONTINUED

LLANGOLLEN & SURROUNDS

The Canal from the Horseshoe Falls to Llangollen Wharf

The starting point for **the Llangollen Canal** is at Llantisilio, about a mile west of Llangollen. It was here in 1806 that Thomas Telford created **the Horseshoe Falls**. This semi-circular basin enabled Telford to divert water from the River Dee to the canal. The natural setting of river, canal, woods and hills make Llantisilio and the Horseshoe Falls a most attractive area. Close by is the interesting 15th century **Llantisilio Church**, which has a beautiful wooden carved roof, an original medieval wooden lectern and some pieces of 15th century stained glass.

From the Horseshoe Falls the infant canal passes a complicated road and rail viaduct system and an ancient chain bridge across the River Dee, as it slowly makes its way to the newly created Llangollen Wharf. From here canal boats can be hired and trips can be taken on the famous Llangollen horsedrawn canal boats.

It is seems strange to look down from the Canal Wharf and to see the station, river and town, which are all at this particular point situated well below the wharf. This is an indication of how much the River Dee has dropped in just one mile, whereas the canal has remained level and so avoiding the use of any locks.

It is from Llangollen Wharf that the Llangollen Canal really begins its 46-mile journey before joining the Shropshire Union Canal at Hursleton Junction. The partially completed Montgomery Canal, coming from near Newtown, joins the Llangollen Canal at Francton Junction.

For the canal journey from Llangollen to Chirk see next page.

Pontcysyllte Aqueduct. *Steel Engraving by E.Finden. 1823*

Chirk Aqueduct. *Steel Engraving by T.Barber.1831.*

TOUR ONE CONTINUED

THE LLANGOLLEN & SURROUNDS

Llangollen Wharf to the Chirk Aqueduct

The four-mile stretch of canal from **Llangollen Wharf to Trevor Wharf** is particularly attractive and makes a fine walk or cycle ride. Trevor Wharf is a busy canal boat centre and the principal stopping place for visitors to Thomas Telford's world famous Pontcysyllte Aqueduct.

The Pontcysyllte Aqueduct is a fantastic piece of waterway engineering as the Llangollen Canal is taken 1007 feet across the Dee valley. This is done at the amazing height of 126 feet above the River Dee and is supported by eighteen elegant arches carrying the huge iron water trough. Work began in 1795 and took ten years to complete. Although the aqueduct is generally attributed to Thomas Telford it was William Jessop who was the chief engineer of the project and constantly advised Telford. The aqueduct was eventually completed in 1805 with great ceremony and at a cost of £27,018.

The Llangollen Canal continues from the Pontcysyllte Aqueduct for about three miles when it reaches the 459 yard long **Chirk tunnel**, which unusually has a towpath running through its entire length. On the other side of the tunnel one comes to a **second impressive aqueduct** which carries the canal 70 feet over the River Ceiriog. **Chirk Aqueduct** was built in 1801 at a cost of £21,000. Running parallel with Telford's aqueduct is the slightly higher railway viaduct, built in 1848, and the two viewed together make a really splendid combination of engineering skills.

The Llangollen Canal continues from Chirk on to Ellesmere and eventually meets the Shropshire Union Canal. However, for the purpose of this tour, we stop at the Chirk Aqueduct.

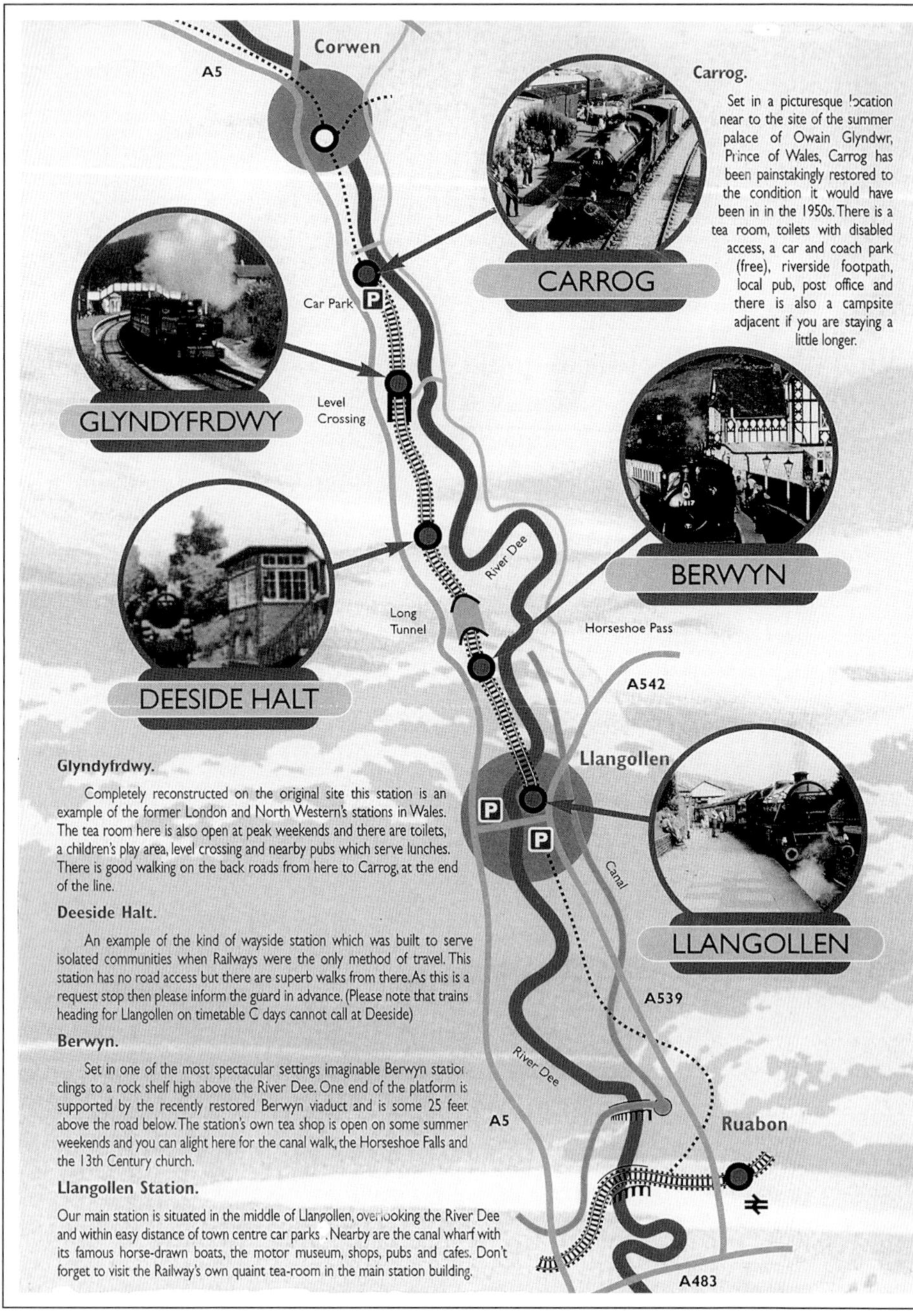

Carrog.

Set in a picturesque location near to the site of the summer palace of Owain Glyndwr, Prince of Wales, Carrog has been painstakingly restored to the condition it would have been in in the 1950s. There is a tea room, toilets with disabled access, a car and coach park (free), riverside footpath, local pub, post office and there is also a campsite adjacent if you are staying a little longer.

Glyndyfrdwy.

Completely reconstructed on the original site this station is an example of the former London and North Western's stations in Wales. The tea room here is also open at peak weekends and there are toilets, a children's play area, level crossing and nearby pubs which serve lunches. There is good walking on the back roads from here to Carrog, at the end of the line.

Deeside Halt.

An example of the kind of wayside station which was built to serve isolated communities when Railways were the only method of travel. This station has no road access but there are superb walks from there. As this is a request stop then please inform the guard in advance. (Please note that trains heading for Llangollen on timetable C days cannot call at Deeside)

Berwyn.

Set in one of the most spectacular settings imaginable Berwyn station clings to a rock shelf high above the River Dee. One end of the platform is supported by the recently restored Berwyn viaduct and is some 25 feet above the road below. The station's own tea shop is open on some summer weekends and you can alight here for the canal walk, the Horseshoe Falls and the 13th Century church.

Llangollen Station.

Our main station is situated in the middle of Llangollen, overlooking the River Dee and within easy distance of town centre car parks . Nearby are the canal wharf with its famous horse-drawn boats, the motor museum, shops, pubs and cafes. Don't forget to visit the Railway's own quaint tea-room in the main station building.

Map of the railway line from Llangollen to Carrog

Reproduced by kind permission of The Llangollen Railway Plc.

TOUR ONE CONTINUED

LLANGOLLEN & SURROUNDS

The Llangollen Railway from Llangollen to Carrog

Llangollen was originally just one of the many stations on the Ruabon to Barmouth line which operated between 1865 and 1968, when it was finally closed as a British Rail line. However, thanks to the enterprise of a large number of steam enthusiasts the eight miles of line between Llangollen and Carrog has been reopened and has proved to be a very popular holiday excursion.

On the journey from Llangollen to Carrog there are three other small stations all of which have been carefully restored to their former use.
Llangollen Station is right in the centre of Llangollen and close to the River Dee on one side and the canal wharf on the other.
Berwyn Station is close to the complicated road viaduct under the railway and over the River Dee. It also has a view of the Horseshoe Falls and the picturesque setting of Llantysilio Church and Hall.
Deeside Halt is just past a huge 'S' shaped bend of the river Dee and gives one a splendid picture of the great beauty of the Vale of the Dee.
Glyndyfrdwy is particularly well known as it is thought that it was the birthplace of Owain Glyndwr, who took his name from this place. A little further down the line, nearer to Carrog, one can see Owain Glyndwr's Mount, where tradition says that in 1400 he declared himself Prince of Wales.
Carrog Station marks the end of the present line where there is an authentic style British Rail refreshment room enabling passengers to buy snacks and drinks, while the engine is put on to the other end of the train. It is hoped that one day the line will be extended from Carrog on to Corwen.

Castell Dinas Bran

Coloured Aquatint by Compte

From an Original Drawing by J.Laporte

c. 1800

The National Library of Wales

TOUR ONE CONTINUED

LLANGOLLEN & SURROUNDS

Castell Dinas Bran

In Simpson's account of the Town and Vale of Llangollen, written in 1837, he writes of **Castell Dinas Bran** as follows:- '*The Castell Dinas Bran, vulgarly called Crow Castle, is one of the primitive Welsh Castles. The Castle stands immediately above and on the north side of Llangollen, on a conical mountain, about seven hundred feet above the level of the Dee, and about one thousand feet above that of the sea; it is built on the summit of the hill, which probably was levelled to procure materials, as the building occupies the whole flat. It seems to have been about hundred yards in length, by fifty yards wide. The present remains are almost without form; they are built of the silicious stone of the mountain, set in a course mortar or grout. There are here and there scattered remains of hewn stone for facings, &c, some vestiges of a small round tower and a vaulted passage.*'

Castell Dinas Bran was constructed in about 1260 by the local Welsh ruler, Prince Gruffudd ap Madoc on the site of a prehistoric hillfort. However, it had a very short life, for in May 1277, during Edward I's initial Welsh campaign, it was deliberately abandoned and fired by its Welsh garrison in order to prevent it being used by the English. In spite of this precaution it was still captured by the English, but they never rebuilt the fortress.

A visit to Castell Dinas Bran is well worth the effort of climbing up the zig zag pathway to the summit. Here the view over Llangollen and the surrounding vale and mountains is spectacular. There are various starting points, but the closest to the town starts from by the school, just above the Canal Wharf.

Trevor Hall with Trevor Rocks in the background

Black and White Copper Engraving

Engraved by J.Walker from an Original Drawing by Evans

1795

END OF TOUR ONE

LLANGOLLEN & SURROUNDS

The Offa's Dyke Path from Trevor Rocks & Eglwyseg Rocks to World's End

From the remains of the Welsh Castle of Dinas Bran there is a superb view of the dramatic mountain range on the opposite side of the valley. This distinctive rocky limestone scarp runs roughly south-east (Trevor Rocks) to north-west (Eglwyseg Rocks). The Offa's Dyke Path runs virtually parallel with these rocks, just below their extraordinary steep scarp.

These two sets limestone scarps form part of a belt of limestone running south-east to north-west of the area, having been laid down 340 million years ago in warm shallow seas. The whole scarp is an area of geological interest, and is now treated as a site of special scientific interest and considered by many to be one of the most impressive limestone scarps in Britain.

There are two main routes to Eglwyseg & Trevor Rocks.

The first route is for a closer view of the Eglwyseg Rocks. This involves a drive or walk from Pentrefelin along the Offa's Dyke Path to what is charmingly called World's End. It also passes the carefully restored Tudor Manor House, situated just before a conveniently placed parking place at World's End.

The second route is for a closer view of the Trevor Rocks. This involves a drive or walk from Trevor to Garth, past the monument to the Welsh Poet Isaac Daniel Hooson (1880-1948) and along the Panorama Walk until it meets the road that goes to World's End.

TOUR TWO

NORTH WEST FROM LLANGOLLEN

Valle Crucis Abbey

Eliseg's Pillar

Horseshoe Pass

Castell Rhodwdd, near Llandegla

Llanarmon-yn-lil Church, Motte & Bailey

Llanfair Dyffryn Clwyd Church

Ruthin Church & Castle

Llanrhaeadr Church, Well & Spring

St Marcella's Parish Church, near Denbigh

Denbigh Castle & Town Walls

Lord Leicester's Church, Denbigh

Denbigh Friary

St Asaph Cathedral

Rhuddlan Castle & Twt Hill Motte & Bailey

Dyserth Waterfall & Church

****

Eliseg's Pillar

Black and White Etching

Engraver and artist not known

1895

START OF TOUR TWO

NORTH WEST FROM LLANGOLLEN

Via Valle Crucis Abbey & Eliseg's Pillar

This tour begins at Llangollen on the A542 road from the town going to the Horseshoe Pass. The beautifully sited Valle Crucis Abbey is about two miles along this road, where the best view of the ruins, with Castell Dinas Bran in the background, is from the hill opposite the main entrance to the Abbey.

Valle Crucis Abbey is the best preserved medieval monastery in North Wales and takes its name '*The Vale of the Cross'* from the ancient **Cross Pillar of Eliseg,** which can be seen in a field just the north of the Abbey. This pillar originally stood 20 feet high and was surmounted with a cross. It was erected in the 7th century by Cyngen (the last independent king of Powys) and was in memory of his great grandfather King Eliseg, who recaptured the land of Powys from the English.

The Abbey was founded by Madoc ap Gruffydd in 1201, for the Cistercian 'White Monks' who set up a community here following the strict rules of their order. The shell of the cross-shaped abbey church is nearly complete, with a splendid west front, which has a triple lancet window, with a rose window above it and the west door below. The east front is also almost complete and has a fine set of five lancet windows. At the far end of the abbey grounds the original monks' fishpond is still well preserved. After a fire in the 15th century many of the buildings were rebuilt, particularly the more elaborate domestic buildings reflecting the growth of wealth in the community at that time and before the dissolution of the Abbey in 1538. These later domestic buildings included a sacristy, a library, a chapter house, which, still has its original ribbed roof vaulting and traceried windows, and above this the monks dormitory.

Valle Crucis Abbey is now in the care of CADW, who have produced an excellent comprehensive guidebook to the Abbey.

TOUR TWO CONTINUED

NORTH WEST FROM LLANGOLLEN

The Horseshoe Pass, Castell y Rhodwydd, Llanarmon yn-Ial & Llanfair Dyffryn Clwyd

From Valle Crucis one proceeds up the dramatic **Horseshoe Pass**, passing on the left the remains of former slate quarries. Towards the highest point of the Pass there are some magnificent views to be seen. These views include Eglwyseg Mountain on the right and on the left, just past the stone quarry, there are good views in the distance towards '*Snowdon's mountain without its people'*, one of the seven wonders of Wales and the only one not in North East Wales.

From the Horseshoe Pass one continues on to Llandegla, near which can be seen the splendid motte and bailey of **Castell y Rhodwydd**, commanding an ideal strategic position for a former Welsh castle. (NB this is on the land belonging to the farm). It is one of the finest medieval earthworks in Wales and was raised by Owain Gwynedd during his conquest of Powys in 1148. Originally the earthen motte would have been topped with a wooden tower and a wooden stockade would have encircled the enclosure.

From Castell y Rhodwydd one can take a diversion to **Llanarmon-yn-Ial,** in order to visit the interesting church set in a spacious churchyard. This church has a superb 18 branch chandelier and some fine tombs. Near the church is the 11th century motte and bailey of Tomen-Y-Faerdre. From Llarmon-yn-lil one has to go across country to visit another fine church at **Llanfair Dyffryn Clwyd.** This church has two wooden carved roofs, part of a medieval rood screen and a splendid monument to a 14th century knight, David ap Madoc. In the south aisle one of the windows contains some interesting remains of 16th century stained glass, thought to have originally come from the east window above the altar. In the churchyard there is the stump of an ancient preaching cross and a very pleasant Georgian vestry house.

Valle Crucis Abbey, with Dinas Bran in the background

Coloured Aquatint by P.Sandby

c.1796

The National Library of Wales

Castell y Rhodwydd, near Llandegla

Photograph by Diana Coleridge

2004

Ruthin, Denbighshire

Copper Engraving by W.Poole

From an Original Drawing by Edward Pugh

1796

TOUR TWO CONTINUED

NORTH WEST FROM LLANGOLLEN

Ruthin Church & Ruthin Castle

From Llanfair Dyffryn Clwyd the tour continues along the A525 to the charming town of **Ruthin**, which has several interesting buildings grouped around St Peter's Square. Foremost amongst these is the 14th century **Parish Church of St Peter**, with its elaborate wrought iron churchyard gates. In 1310 Lord Grey of Ruthin created a collegiate church here, and the incumbent is still known as 'The Warden'. The choir was destroyed in 1663 and the spire was added in 1859. *(Note that the 1796 engraving opposite, shows the church without the spire).* The two roofs are particularly splendid, especially the one in the north aisle, *(formally the nave),* which has over 400 carved panels and was given by King Henry VII as a thank offering to the people of Wales. Outside the church, on the north side, one can still see the remains of the collegiate cloisters, which are now part of the Warden's home.

South east of the Parish Church is **Ruthin Castle,** now a modern hotel. (*Access to the gardens and the remains of the original medieval castle must be obtained from the hotel.*) The first castle was probably early Norman. In 1277 Edward I granted the site to Dafydd, brother of Llewelyn the Last, who undoubtedly did some rebuilding. However, in 1282 when Dafydd supported his brother's uprising, Ruthin Castle was taken for Edward I by Reginald de Grey who set about building the rectangular fortress which survives as today's ruin. During the Civil War Ruthin became a garrison for Charles I but was retaken by General Mytton and dismantled in 1647. In the 1826 part of the castle remains were converted into a two-storied house and in 1849 this was demolished and the present three-storied red sandstone house was erected with an octagonal tower in the mock gothic style, and is now the Ruthin Castle Hotel.

TOUR TWO CONTINUED

NORTH WEST FROM LLANGOLLEN

St Dyfnog's Church, Llanrhaeadr & St Marcella's Parish Church

This tour continues along the A525 from the attractive town of Ruthin via two superb medieval churches. The first is just off the A525 at Llanrhaeadr. The second is St Marcella's Parish Church or Eglwys Wen, a mile east of Denbigh and on the minor road just off the roundabout on the A525.

Llanrhaeadr-yng-Nghinmeirch *or 'The church of the waterfall in the district of Cinmeirch'* has one of the finest medieval parish churches in Wales. It gets its long Welsh name from the tradition that Dyfnog, a 6th century hermit, lived here and set up his cell beside a holy well and close to the small waterfall, just below the natural springs. A stone bath now marks this holy site and is used by pilgrims who come here for healing.

The double-naved church of St Dyfnog, with its grand hammer beam roofs, is full of wonderful treasures of which the most obvious is the large brilliantly coloured Jesse window (1533), considered by many as the finest stained glass window in Wales. There are also further remains of glass (1508) in the window over the vestry. The 16th century. golden pelican feeding her young with her own blood, an ancient Eucharistic symbol, is particularly fine, as is the elaborately carved timber porch.

St Marcella's (Llanfarchell) Church, although over a mile **from** Denbigh, is still regarded as Denbigh Parish Church. The church is named after its patroness, Marchell the Virgin, who is thought to have set up her hermitage here beside a holy well in the 7th century. It is also a doubled- naved church with a very fine 15th century hammer-beam roof. Around the twin altars are a number of exquisite monuments depicting various local Elizabethan gentry.

NB. This church is only open on Saturday mornings from Easter to October.

END OF TOUR TWO

NORTHWEST FROM LLANGOLLEN

Denbigh Castle, Lord Leicester's Church & Denbigh Friary

This second tour continues northwards with a visit to the **historic town of Denbigh**. Denbigh is dominated by the steep rocky outcrop on which the castle and old town were built. This site was once the residence of the Welsh Princes, but in 1282 it was superseded by the present castle, built for Henry de Lacey, Earl of Lincoln, having been given the site by King Edward I.
Denbigh Castle consisted of a strong enclosure wall with seven towers, a massive gatehouse and town walls. On the south and west sides, where the slopes are steep, the towers are smaller but on the north and east sides, facing the town and flatter, the towers are polygonal and much stronger. Denbigh castle was never intended to stand in isolation and de Lacey also founded a fortified town within the town walls. At Denbigh these **fortified walls** were over 1200 yards long and had four towers and two gateways. One gateway (the Burgess Gate) still survives as does much of the wall. The St Hilary Tower, standing alone, is all that remains of the former parish church for those within the walls.

Near the castle walls can be seen the remains of **Lord Leicester's Church.** Robert Dudley, Earl of Leicester and Lord of Denbigh decided to build a new church that was fitting to his status as virtual governor of North Wales, and also possibly to replace St Asaph's Cathedral. This was begun in 1578 and was built up to roof height but was never completed.

On the outskirts of the town, almost hidden away, are the remains of **Denbigh Friary**. This was a former Carmelite or White Friars Friary founded in the late 13th century. All that remains today are the greater part of the original church walls. The roof was destroyed by fire in1899.

Denbigh Castle & Friary & Leicester's Church

Hand coloured Copper Engraving by Sparrow

1786

St Dyfnog's Church, Llanrhaeadr

16th Century Jesse Window

Photograph by Diana Coleridge

2004

St Asaph Catheral

Black & White Vignette Steel Engraving

Published by T.Catherall, Chester

c.1860

TOUR TWO CONTINUED

NORTH WEST FROM LLANGOLLEN

St Asaph Cathedral

From Denbigh Castle it is only a short drive to three more exciting attractions. The first of these is **St Asaph Cathedral,** which has been a site of Christian worship since AD 560 and was founded by St Kentigern. Asaph, who gave his name to the city and to the diocese, succeeded Bishop Kentigern in 570.

'The present building, mainly 13th century, is a mixture of architecture dating from the 13th – 14th centuries, giving a blend of simplicity, quiet dignity and beauty.'

The stained glass was destroyed in the 17th century, much of which was replaced in the late 19th century. The west window is 20th century and is a memorial to the first Archbishop of Wales. **The roof** is much later than the rest of the building and was restored and decorated in 1968. **The Presbytery**, the area east of the choir, contains the Bishop's Throne. Beneath the throne is the burial place of **Bishop William Morgan**, who translated the bible into Welsh in 1588 and was Bishop of St Asaph from1601-1604. The finely carved stalls date from 1482. This area was much restored by Gilbert Scott in 1869-1875. There are two chapels, T**he Translators Chapel** on the north, commemorating the men responsible for the translation the bible into Welsh in the 16th & 17th centuries, and **The Lady Chapel** on the South, dating from 1336 and houses a 16th century Spanish Madonna.

Outside the Cathedral one can clearly see how two different types of stone have been used for building the cathedral. The fine-grained limestone came from the quarries at Cefn, and the sandstone from Flint or Talacre. This is a curious combination of stone as the two react chemically with each other and are gradually wearing each other away!

Rhuddlan Castle

Black & White Steel Engraving

Engraved by E. Finden

From an Original Drawing by Captain Batty

1823

TOUR TWO CONTINUED

NORTH EAST FROM LLANGOLLEN

Rhuddlan Castle & Twthill Motte & Bailey

From St Asaph it is only a short run northwards to Rhuddlan, which means 'the red bank' because of the colour of its riverside soil. The principal glory of **Rhuddlan** is its superb castle, standing proud over the River Clwyd, where there was an ancient crossing of the river.

Rhuddlan was the first of Edward I's concentric castles on the north Welsh coast, and was followed by the castles at Conwy, Harlech and Beaumaris. These castles consist of three concentric rings of fortification rather than the traditional keep. The innermost of this fortification consists of a diamond-plan strong hold, with a twin-towered gatehouse at two corners and a single round tower at the others. Beyond this is there is an outer circuit of lower turreted walls, and beyond this a deep moat which was linked with the River Clwyd. The castle is now in the care of CADW, who have produced an excellent guidebook to the castle.

By an amazing piece of engineering the river Clwyd was converted into a two-mile deep-water channel to the sea so that Edward I's ships could relieve the castle at times of siege. Once this channel was completed Rhuddlan Castle then became the base for Edward's decisive invasion of Wales in 1282.

A short way from Rhuddlan castle is a way-marked footpath to **Twthill motte and bailey,** which was once the site of the Norman precursor to Edward I's castle. The motte would have had a timber tower and was built in 1073 by Robert of Rhuddlan on possibly the former site of a Welsh palace. At its foot was a stockaded enclosure, and beyond that a ditched Norman town, with its own Dominican priory.

Dyserth Waterfall

Black & White Vignette, Steel Engraving

Newman & Co, published by D.L.Lewis of Rhyl

c.1870

END OF TOUR TWO

NORTH EAST FROM LLANGOLLEN

Dyserth Waterfall, Parish Church & Castle

From Rhuddlan one takes the A5155 to the village of Dyserth where there are three main attractions to be seen. These are the waterfall, the parish church and the site of the castle.

The waterfall at Dyserth is right in the centre of the village, an area which is full of healthy springs in the limestone uplands above the village. It is these springs, rather than the small river that produce the fairly constant flow of water in the fall. At one time there was a working mill built near the fall and one can still see the evidence of this mill.

On the left of the fall is the interesting **church of St. Bridget and St. Cwyfan.** The church has obviously been a place of Christian worship for many centuries as demonstrated by the discovery of a large Celtic 11th century churchyard cross, which is now inside the church. However the main attraction of the church is the superb medieval stained glass east window where the top part (c.1450) depicts the twelve apostles and the main section is of 'a Jesse Tree' (c.1530) depicting the lineage of Christ from Jesse, the father of King David.

A mile and a half north-east of the village can be seen the site of the former **Dyserth Castle**, built by the English in 1241. Originally it would have complemented and have been similar to the motte and bailey of Twthill, beside Rhuddlan Castle (see previous page). The castle was soon destroyed by Llywelyn, the last of the Princes of Gwynedd, and very little has survived the ravages of time.

TOUR THREE

NORTH EAST FROM LLANGOLLEN

Overton Parish Church

Wrexham Parish Church

Gresford Parish Church

Caergwrle Castle – Welsh

Hawarden Castle - English

Ewloe Castle - Welsh

Flint Castle – English

St Winefride's Well, Holywell

Basingwerk Abbey

The Clywedog Valley Trail, Minera to Bersham

The Clywedog Valley Trail, Bersham to Kings Mill

Erddig House & Gardens - National Trust

Overton Church

Overton Yew Trees, one of the Seven Wonders of Wales,
as are Wrexham Steeple & Gresford Bells

Black & White Steel Engraving
Drawn by H.Gastineau & Engraved by W.Ratclyffe

1836

Wrexham Church. *Wood Engraving by H.Hughes. 1823*

Gresford Church. *Wood Engraving by H.Hughes. 1823*

TOUR THREE CONTINUED

NORTH EAST FROM LLANGOLLEN

Overton, Wrexham and Gresford Parish Churches

The three great Parish churches of Overton, Wrexham and Gresford are all included in the rhyme '*The Seven Wonders of Wales*', a title that all three churches richly deserve.

St Mary's, Overton is remembered for its ancient **yew trees,** some of which are thought to date back 1500-2000 years. The church tower is 14th century and houses a set of six bells and a clock. The Norman circle cross, built into the west pillar of the church is thought to be the oldest stonework in the church. Also look out for the 15th century oak chest and a 6th century Abyssinian brass processional cross.

St Giles, Wrexham, set in the centre of the busy county town, is remembered for its superb **steeple or tower**. This 147 feet tower was begun in 1506 and has four graceful hexagonal turrets and a number of medieval carvings of its patron saint St Giles. The pillars, arches and corbels in the nave were built in the 14th century, however in the 15th century the church was heightened and given present clear storey, carved roof. and a large east window. This east window was later altered and made into an entrance arch into the chancel. Wrexham church is well known to Americans, as it is the burial place of Elihu Yale (1648-1720) the founder of Yale University.

All Saints Gresford is remembered for its **bells** and is considered by many to be the finest parish church in Wales. The church possesses a multitude of treasures, including a particularly fine tower, which houses the famous bells, a fine timbered roof and some excellent stained glass. The reason for this wealth of possessions was largely due to the many pilgrims who used to flock to Gresford Church to visit an image, probably of the Virgin Mary, which was thought to have miraculous powers. This image was removed at the reformation and the pilgrims and their money ceased.

Caergwrle Castle. *Steel Engraving by J.M.Starling.1831*

Hawarden Castle. *Soft Ground Etching by J.G.Wood. 1813*

TOUR THREE CONTINUED

NORTH EAST FROM LLANGOLLEN

Caergwrle Welsh Castle & Hawarden (Old) English Castle

From Gresford church the tour continues either along the B5373 to ***Caergwrle Castle,*** *or along the A550 to* ***Hawarden Castle****, both of which have historic links with each other.*

Caergwrle Castle, the last of the Welsh castles, was built in 1277 by Dafydd ap Gruffudd, the younger brother of Prince Llywelyn. Dafydd had allied himself with Edward I and was rewarded with the land and probably the workforce to build Caergwrle Castle. However in 1282 Dafydd attacked Hawarden Castle, which sparked off a new Anglo-Welsh war. The result was that Edward's troops attacked Caergwrle Castle but found Dafydd gone and the castle in ruins. Edward set about rebuilding the castle and in 1283 gave it to Queen Eleanor with the new name of Hope Castle. Today the ruins of castle, built on the site of an older hillfort, are in a poor state of repair. However, one can still see the remains of the distinctive D-shaped Welsh north tower, commanding superb views over the countryside.

Dafydd attacked **Hawarden Castle** because it was a strategically placed Borderland castle on the main road from Chester to North Wales which until 1804, literally passed beneath its ramparts. Hawarden Castle was built on an ancient hillfort, which was re-used for the Norman motte and bailey built by Hugh, the Earl of Chester. In 1265 Prince Llywelyn destroyed this castle. In 1282 a new English castle was begun to be built which prompted the attack by Dafydd. Today the castle remains, with its splendidly preserved keep, are in private ownership and can only be visited when the gardens of the crenellated mansion are open. This mansion was once the home of Prime Minister William Gladstone and now of his descendants.

Ewloe Castle. *Drawn & Etched by J.Bailey 1835*

Flint Castle, *Steel Engraving by S. Lacey 1831*

TOUR THREE CONTINUED

NORTH EAST FROM LLANGOLLEN

Ewloe Welsh Castle & Flint English Castle

*From Harwarden Castle the tour continues along the B5125 to Ewloe and **Ewloe Castle** is a mile beyond the village on the right and in the woods. **Flint Castle** is north west of Ewloe on the mouth of the River Dee*

Ewloe Castle is beautifully situated in the corner of a small wood, which originally was part of the great Forest of Ewloe. It is the oldest surviving stone castle in the Borderlands and the best preserved of the castles that were built by the Welsh Princes, having been built c.1257 by Prince Llywelyn ap Gruffudd. The castle consists of two wards. **The upper ward is** built on a natural outcrop and it surrounds a rectangular keep, with a traditional Welsh D-shaped apsidal eastern end. **A lower ward** encloses a well and a western round tower. After the Edwardian Conquest in 1277, and the building of Flint Castle in its final form, Ewloe ceased to be of strategic importance and fell into disuse.

Flint Castle stands imposingly on the banks of the Dee shoreline and was the first of the chain of castles built by Edward I. This was done by Edward I in order to defeat Prince Llywelyn and to halt his rugged determination for Welsh independence. Work on Flint Castle began in 1277 and was virtually finished by 1284. It consisted of a **four-square ward with four round towers,** one of which was much larger than the others, and had its own moat and drawbridge dominating the entrance to the castle. In 1399 Flint Castle was the final refuge of Richard II before he conceded the crown to Henry IV. It changed hands several times during the Civil War and finally fell to Parliament in 1646 and then into disuse.

CADW have produced an excellent one volume guide to both Ewloe and Flint Castles.

St. Winefride's Well. *Steel Engraving by W.Wallis. 1836*

Basingwerk Abbey. *Copper Engraving by J.Caldwell. 1790*

TOUR THREE CONTINUED

NORTH EAST FROM LLANGOLLEN

St Winefride's Well, Holywell & Basingwerk Abbey

From Flint Castle it is only a short journey along the A548 to St Winefrede's Well at Holywell and the ruins of a former Abbey at Basingwerk, set in the Greenfield Valley Heritage Park, and marks the northernmost part of this tour.

Wales has many Holy Wells, which in the past were much visited as places of healing and prayer. This was, and still is, particularly true of **St Winefride's Well,** from which the town of Holywell takes its name, and is included as one more of *'The Seven Wonders of Wales'*. The origins of the well, according to legend, go back to the 7th century when a rejected suitor beheaded the Welsh Princess Gwefrewi (Winefride). The head, legend says, bounced down the hill to a spring. Her uncle St Beuno then picked it up and replaced the head on her neck and so restored Winefride's life for another 15 years. A shrine was then built on the spot and throughout the Middle Ages pilgrims flocked here for healing. In about 1500 Margaret Beaufort, the mother of Henry VII, rebuilt the shrine to its present splendour. Even after the Reformation the shrine became, as it still does, a place of pilgrimage and healing.

A little further down the road and near the coast at Greenfield can be seen the ruins of the former **Basingwerk Abbey**. Ranulph, Earl of Chester, founded Basingwerk Abbey in 1131 as a house of the Savignac Order, but in 1147 it became a Cistercian house. At the reformation the buildings were largely demolished and sold. The timber roof the choir went to St Mary's on the Hill in Chester, that of the refectory possibly to Cilcain, and the stained glass possibly to Dyserth. Today the best remains can be seen in the west wall, one of the crossing piers and in the monk's domestic buildings. In the refectory one can still see the remains of the former reader's pulpit. The ruins are now in the care of CADW Welsh Historic Monuments who have produced a guidebook to the Abbey.

TOUR THREE CONTINUED

NORTH EAST FROM LLANGOLLEN

The Clywedog Valley

From Minera to Bersham (via Nant Mill)

Either from Llangollen take the attractive minor road to Minera, via World's End (see p.25), or from the Wrexham by-pass (A543) take the turning off to Bersham, where there is a convenient parking place near the Heritage Centre.

From Bersham there is a valley Trail which runs three miles to the west to Minera and two and a half miles to the east to King's Mill. This trail has a waymarked path along the valley which was once the scene of heavy industry but now a peaceful area, where one can enjoy the beauty of the natural river scenery, within the setting of former industry, in four easy stages.

Stage one is from Minera to Nant Mill (1.5 miles) and is the site of the former lead mines that abounded in the Minera area of the valley. The name 'Minera' comes from the Latin word for ore, a reminder that mining here probably goes back to Roman times and finally reached its zenith in 1847. At Minera one can still see how the former **City Engine House** used to pump water from the mines down to the **Deep Dry Level,** near Nant Mill.

Stage two is from Nant Mill to Bersham (1.5 miles). At Nant there is a fine restored former **Fulling Mill**, used for thickening cloth, but by the late 18th century it had become a **Corn Mill** and is now a visitor's centre and is the haunt of various species of bats. Going down stream one passes a 19th century gothic bridge, two weirs, the remains of sluice gates and a dry leate, all of which were used to supply a steady flow of water to the ironworks in this area.

TOUR THREE CONTINUED

NORTH EAST FROM LLANGOLLEN

The Clywedog Valley continued

Bersham to King's Mill (via Felin Puleston)

Stage three is from Bersham to Felin Puleston. At Bersham there were formerly two iron works used for making cannon and steam engines, the ore having come from Minera. The first was at **Bersham Mill**, which was built as an iron foundry and then, when it was closed, was converted into a corn mill. The second was **'The East Ironworks'** which, when it was closed, became first a school and then the present excellent Heritage Centre. A little further down stream is a weir providing a steady flow of water for the former **'Turkey Paper Mill'**, which used to make high quality hand made paper for bank notes and cheque books etc.

Stage four is from Felin Puleston to King's Mill. Felin Puleston is now an educational centre, but originally the buildings were first a mill and then a tenanted farm on the Erddig estate. Near the bridge there are a weir and an old millstone in the Sensory Garden which are all that remains of the former **16th century Felin Puleston Corn Mill**. Further down stream was the much older and more important **14th century King's Mill**, which had the monopoly on milling in the area. There was always great competition between these two mills until 1769, when Philip Yorke of Erddig rebuilt King's Mill and converted Puleston Mill to farm use.

This final stage of the Clywedog Valley is also part of the large Erddig estate and is in the care of the National Trust (see P.59). The natural lake between the two mills was formed due to subsidence from the former coal mines that lie beneath the surface.

Wrexham County Borough has produced an excellent guide to the Clywedog Valley. especially for those who want to walk along the trail..

Engine House at Minera Lead Mine, Clywedog Valley

Nant Mill Visitor Centre, Clywedog Valley
Photographs by Diana Kingston 2005

Bersham Mill, Clywedog Valley

Felin Puleston, Clywedog Valley

Photographs by Diana Kingston 2005

Erddig, Denbighshire

Copper Engraving by Medland

From an Original Drawing by Evans

1792

THE END OF TOUR THREE

NORTH EAST FROM LLANGOLLEN

Erddig House and Garden

From the King's Mill it is only a short way to Erddig House & Garden, carefully following the well marked National Trust signs.

The original house at **Erddig** (the present central bays) was built between 1684-87 but turned out to be a financial disaster for the owner, Joshua Edisbury, who fled to London where he died c.1715 before the house was finished. In 1716 John Meller, a London lawyer, acquired Erddig. It was Meller who added the two wings and collected most of the fine furniture that is still in the house today. Simon Yorke, the nephew of Meller, also assisted in this restoration and he inherited Erddig in 1733. It then remained in direct line with the Yorke family until 1973, when it was given to the National Trust, who began a mammoth and very successful restoration campaign.

One of the attractions of Erddig is that the National Trust has more or less left the contents of the house and outbuildings as they were when they inherited it from the Yorke family. The result is that one is given a clear picture of life in a country house in the early 20th century. It also reflects the care that the Yorke family had for their considerable domestic and estate staff.

The National Trust has also restored the **gardens at Erddig** to their former Edwardian glory. These gardens include the formal parterre, the axial walk, the rose garden, the fishpond, the canal and screen, a moss and a yew walk and an herb border. There are also superb examples of espaliers, or fans, of old varieties of fruit trees and avenues of pleached limes.

For full details of the house and garden see the National Trust guide book.

TOUR FOUR

SOUTH FROM LLANGOLLEN

FOUR BORDER CASTLES

Chirk Castle – English

Powis Castle - Welsh & English

Dolforwyn Castle – Welsh

Montgomery Castle - English

The White Baroque Wrought Iron Gates at Chirk Castle

Made in 1719 by the 'Davies' brothers

Photograph by Diana Coleridge

2005

Chirk Castle

Black & White Steel Engraving

Engraved by J.C.Varrall

From an Original Drawing by H. Gastineau

1831

THE START OF TOUR FOUR
SOUTH FROM LLANGOLLEN

Chirk Castle

From Llangollen take the A5(T) south to the junction with the B5070 to Chirk. In Chirk turn right at the war memorial, carved and engraved by Eric Gill, and then follow the National Trust signs for Chirk Castle.

A mile from Chirk one comes to the fine **baroque wrought iron gates,** at the entrance to the **Chirk Castle estate,** which were made in 1719 by the two 'Davies' blacksmith brothers from Bersham. Beyond the gates mature trees border the drive to the castle but there is no sign of the castle until near the car park, where one can see it standing proud against a backdrop of the local hills.

Chirk Castle is a genuine medieval castle whose exterior has not changed much since it was built, except that the arrow slits have been enlarged into mullioned windows. During the War of the Roses and in the Civil War it was badly damaged but was repaired again after both occasions. Roger Mortimer began building the castle in 1295 and it was eventually completed in 1310 when it became the home of many powerful landowners, one of whom was Robert Dudley, Earl of Leicester. In 1595 the estate was bought by the prosperous goldsmith Sir Thomas Myddelton of Denbigh and it has remained the Myddleton Family home ever since. It is now in the care of the National Trust. A moat, drawbridge and portcullis once protected the castle but these have now virtually gone, however evidence of the former portcullis can be seen in the groves cut into the gateway.

Chirk Castle also has **a fine garden** with superb sweet smelling climbers on the walls, topiary yews planted in the 1870's, herbaceous borders, a rock garden and many grand trees as well as a **460 acre park**, which is crossed by Offa's Dyke.

For a full guide to the house, garden and park see the comprehensive National Trust guidebook.

Powis Castle

Black & White Copper Engraving

Drawn by Grose & Engraved by White

1813

TOUR FOUR CONTINUED

SOUTH FROM LLANGOLLEN

Powis Castle

From Chirk Castle one returns to the A5 (T) south to the junction with the A483 going south to Welshpool, where there are National Trust signs for Powis Castle on the right.

The Princes of Powys first established **Powis Castle** in the 13th century for two principle reasons**.** First to protect it from the invasion of Wales by Edward I in the east, and secondly to protect it against their rival Welsh Princes of Gwynedd in the west. However, as Edward's grip on North Wales grew stronger and stronger, the last Prince of Powys gave up his princely title and threw in his lot with the English as his best protection against the Princes of Gwynedd. Thus began the massive building plan, which laid the foundations for the present grand castle.

The Castle was built from the craggy outcrop of red gritstone on which it now stands, following the traditional Norman style, with a strong keep (the present castle), an inner bailey (the entrance courtyard) and a massive outer wall. The oldest parts of the castle (c.1200) are **the twin drum towers** at the entrance. Over the last 400 years this former medieval fortress, which originally was built for war, transformed into a sumptuous dwelling place, and became the home of the great Herbert and Clive dynasties, who still live in part of the castle that is now cared for by the National Trust

On the five terraces below the castle are the superb **Powis Castle Gardens**. These gardens combine 18th century lead statues and huge clipped yew trees with various formal gardens, inspired by the baroque gardens of France and Italy. Beyond these formal gardens and surrounding the castle is the ancient wooded deer-park.

For full details of the Castle, its contents, the Clive Museum and the gardens, please refer to the National Trust guidebook.

Dolforwyn Castle

Watercolour by Moses Griffith

1776

The National Library of Wales

TOUR FOUR CONTINUED

SOUTH FROM LLANGOLLEN

Dolforwyn Castle

From Powis Castle one returns to the A483, south for about 10 miles towards Newtown, turning right for Dolforwyn Hall, just before the bridge over the Llangollen Canal and River Severn. Dolforwyn Castle is marked on OS map 136 ref.152950.

Dolforwyn Castle is sited on a rocky platform at the top of a steep ridge overlooking the Severn Valley. It was a Welsh castle, of the Princes of Gwynedd, and fortified by Llywelyn ap Gruffudd in 1273 as a stronghold against both the English and the Princes of Powys. This caused alarm amongst the English who gave orders for the building to stop and when this was ignored the castle was taken by Edward I's troops in 1277. It was then given to Roger III of the powerful Mortimer family. The castle was kept in repair for some years but by 1398 it was in ruins and the small township that Llywelyn had established on the west of the ridge was suppressed and Newtown was founded in 1279 on a more suitable site.

Recently CADW has carried out extensive excavation and repair work, which gives a much more comprehensive plan of the original castle. This consists of rectangular curtain wall, incorporating a D-shaped tower, which surrounds a large rectangular tower at one end and a round tower at the other. Both of these towers are integrated into the rest of the castle buildings, with the main entrance through a simple doorway at the west end of the castle

On the way up to the castle one passes the small cottage which has a massive yew tree, which must date back at least to the 13th century castle standing proudly above it.

For full details see the CADW guidebook for Dolforwyn & Montgomery Castles.

Montgomery Castle

Drawn and Engraved by Samuel & Nathaniel Buck

1742

The National Library of Wales

THE END OF TOUR FOUR

SOUTH FROM LLANGOLLEN

Montgomery Castle

From Dolforwyn Castle one returns to the A483 where one has to turn right over the River Severn and then left again at the junction with the B4386 to Montgomery. The Castle stands high up on the left overlooking the town.

In 1233 the stone built castle, high up and looking down on the town at Montgomery, succeeded the motte and bailey at **Hen Domen**, a mile north west of Montgomery. This first Norman castle was built by Roger de Montgomery, Earl of Shrewsbury, and was named after his ancestral seat in Normandy. The building of the new fortified stone castle at Montgomery began as a result of Henry III's campaign against Llywelyn ap Iorwerth.

The entrance to **Montgomery Castle** is by the modern bridge over an **outer ditch,** leading into the **middle ward**, where there are remains of two round towers, either side of the gatehouse and the curtain wall. Inside the middle ward are good remains of the original kiln house. A second bridge, over **an inner ditch,** leads into the **inner ward,** which also has two round towers, either side of the gatehouse and its curtain wall. Inside the inner ward there is D-shaped tower enclosing the castle well, the remains of the kitchens and brewhouse and a round tower at its far end.

Over the years CADW has carried out a major restoration programme so that the castle is now much more accessible. For full details of Montgomery Castle see the excellent guidebook produced by CADW.

Below Montgomery Castle lies the attractive Georgian styled **town of Montgomery**. The 13th century parish church has a fine double Screen and Loft, part of which is thought to have come from the former Austin Canons Priory at Chirbury, 2.5 miles north east, in England. Offa's Dyke was cut through Montgomery in about 784 and a section of this has been preserved in Lymore Park, east of the town.

TOUR FIVE

SOUTH WEST OF LLANGOLLEN

The Ceiriog Valley (1)
via
Chirk, Pont Faen, Offa's Dyke, Pontfadog & Glyn Ceiriog

The Ceiriog Valley (2)
via
Glyn Ceiriog, Pandy, Tregeiriog & Llanarmon D.C.

A Tour to Pistyll Rhaeadr

A Tour to Pennant Melangell

The Motte & Bailey at Sycharth

Llanarmon Dyffryn Ceiriog

A photograph of a yew tree estimated to be over 1000 years old, St Garmon's Churchyard

(Source unknown)

THE START OF TOUR FIVE

SOUTH WEST OF LLANGOLLEN

The Ceiriog Valley (1)

From Chirk to Glyn Ceiriog

The Chirk and Ceiriog Valley Partnership have produced an excellent illustrated guide to the delightful ***Ceiriog Valley****, which they have broken into seven easy stages. However for the purpose of this book only the very basic details are given with some of the points of interest that can be seen on the way.*

Stage One is from Chirk to Pont Faen. This includes the Chirk aqueduct and viaduct (see page 12), Chirk Castle Woods and the stone bridge at Pont Faen.

Stage Two is from Pont Faen to Offa's Dyke. This includes woods belonging to the Woodland Trust, good views of Chirk Castle and at Castle Mill the opportunity to cross Offa's Dyke, the remarkable historic 168 miles of earthen bank dividing England and Wales.

Stage Three is from Offa's Dyke to Pontfadog. This section includes a hillside walk above the valley with splendid views to the north and to the east. Near the river bank there are remains of the kilns used in the lime mining industry and at Pontfadog one can visit the Tramway Waiting Room where there are details of the former Glyn Valley Tramway which was closed in 1935.

Stage Four is from Pontfadog to Glyn Ceiriog. This particular area of the Ceiriog valley was once a slate mining and flannel milling district, but is now an area of attractive meadows and woodlands. At Glyn Ceiriog, the largest settlement in the valley, there are many signs of the rich cultural and religious heritage of this district, demonstrated by its many churches, chapels and by the Eisteddfod circle of 'Gorsedd' stones in the playing field.

TOUR FIVE CONTINUED

SOUTH WEST OF LLANGOLLEN

The Ceiriog Valley (2)

From Glyn Ceiriog to Llanarmon Dyffryn Ceiriog

Stage Five is from Glyn Ceiriog to Pandy. This is an area that is rich in wildlife and is dominated by Craig y Pandy, (1165 feet) the highest point of the walk. It is also an area of geological importance, having a variety of mineral deposits, including slate, silica, granite and china stone. By the road one can still see the flooded caverns of the former mining areas.

Stage Six is from Pandy to Tregeiriog. Pandy is the Welsh for fulling mill and is named after the mill (now the Woolpack Inn) that used to be here turning wool into flannel, using fullers earth. At Hendre there was a huge quarry providing dolerite, a stone similar to granite used in road building and for stone facing. This was the furthest point of the tram railway, part of which has been preserved by the National Trust.

Stage Seven is from Tregeiriog to Llanarmon Dyffryn Ceiriog. Llanarmon D.C, as it is often called, was the stopping point for the drovers on their way to England. The translation into English is *'The Church of St Armon in the wide valley of the Ceiriog'*. The local church of St Garmon has at least one yew tree that is over 1000 years old and near the churchyard gate there is a preaching mound pre-dating any church building. In the 1920s there were plans to flood this area in order to create two reservoirs but fortunately these plans were abandoned.

From the Ceiriog Valley and Llanarmon DC one has to go south via various minor roads in order to get to Llanrhaeadr-ym-Mochnant and the Rhaeadr Valley.

Porch at Glyn Ceiriog

Watercolour by the Revd. John Parker

1811

The National Library of Wales

St. Armon's Church

Llanarmon Dyffryn Ceiriog

Photograph by Diana Coleridge

2005

Pistyll Rhaeadr

Black and White Copper Engraving

From the Gentleman's Magazine

January 1750

TOUR FIVE CONTINUED

SOUTH WEST OF LLANGOLLEN

Side roads to Pistyll Rhaeadr from Llanarmon D.C.

From Llanarmon Dyffryn Ceiriog it is possible to take a number of side roads southwards across the edge of the Berwyn Mountains to the village of ***Llanrhaeadr-ym-Mochnant.*** *This is not a route that is practical to describe in detail but is clearly marked on the Ordnance Survey Explorer Map 155.*

Llanrhaeadr-ym-Mochnant is particularly well known as being the village where the scholarly Dr William Morgan was once the vicar. In 1588 Doctor Morgan wrote the first translation of the Bible into Welsh and in 1595 was offered the Bishopric of Llandaff and in 1599 was translated to St Asaph, where he died in 1604. In the church there is a Celtic slab cross dating back to the 9th-10th century.

From the Church one follows the narrow road north west for about four miles to the parking place provided for those visiting the celebrated **Pistyll Rhaeadr**, the highest waterfall in Wales and another of '*The seven wonders of Wales*'. Thomas Compton in 1817 describes the fall as follows. '*The height of the fall is said to be about 210 feet, but has the appearance of being more. It is broken at about two thirds of this distance from the top, and falls into a small but deep black basin, in the mouth of which, the water, by washing through the interstices of the rock, has gradually worn it away, leaving a natural arch, under which, the whole water of the fall now rushes, and is then again precipitated into a chasm below*'.

At the bottom of the fall there is a narrow bridge which enables one to climb up to the top of the fall and to have a splendid view of the lush valley below. The fall is fed by the tiny River Disgynfa and it is amazing to see how such a small river can produce such a fine fall, which after heavy rain is a fantastic sight and well worth the long journey to visit it in all its natural glory.

St Melangell Church, Pennant Melangell

Watercolour by John Ingleby

c.1794

The National Library of Wales

THE END OF TOUR FIVE

SOUTH WEST OF LLANGOLLEN

From Llanrhaeadr-ym-Mochnant to Pennant Melangell & Sycharth

From Llanrhaeadr-ym-Mochnant take the minor roads to Penybontfawr and follow the B4391 to Llangynog, where one bears left and follow the River Tanat to ***Pennant Melangell****.*

Llangynog, a former lead mining area, gets its name from Cynog, son of a 5th century prince, and is a spread out village beautifully set below the Berwyn mountains at the junction of the Eirth and Tanat valleys.

After two miles along the charming wooded valley of the Upper Tanat one reaches the small Norman Church of **Pennant Melangell**. Inside the church there are two 14th century recumbent effigies, one said to be that of a Welsh prince and the other of **St Melangell**. The church also has a fine 18th century pulpit, a medieval font and an early 15th century rood screen, depicting the 8th century legend of St Melangell, an Irish princess, who retreated to this place for a life of contemplation. Apparently a hare that was being hunted by Brochwel, the Prince of Powis, escaped by taking refuge under the robe of Melangell. The Prince in recognition of her holiness gave her the land on which she then founded her monastery. As a result of this Melangell became the patron saint of hares, affectionately known as '*St Melangell's Lambs*' and treated as being sacred in the locality. **St Melangell's shrine (**Bell-y-Bedd) became a place of pilgrimage in the Middle Ages and the present church was built at one end of the shrine. The shrine has been carefully restored and is still a place of pilgrimage.

From Pennant Melangell it is worth while taking a short detour to the hamlet of **Sycharth** (OS.205 259). Here there is a large motte and bailey, which marks the site of a former principle residence of Owain Glyndwr and was sadly destroyed in1403 by the English.

(*NB The motte & bailey are on private land, belonging to the adjacent farm).*

TOUR SIX

WEST OF LLANGOLLEN

THE A5 TO PONT Y GLYN-DIFFWYS

The King's Bridge over the River Dee
the Berwyn Railway Viaduct

Glyndyfrdwy, Owain Glyndwr's Mound
Corwen Church & Town

Rug Chapel & Visitor's Centre (CADW)

Diversion to Llangar Church (CADW)

The Waterfall at Cynwyd & Pont y Glyn-diffwys

Rug Chapel

One of the coloured wooden roof carvings

Photograph by Cadw.

The Bridge over the River Dee & the Railway Viaduct
at Berwyn, near Llangollen

Photograph Diana Coleridge

2004

THE START OF TOUR SIX

WEST OF LLANGOLLEN

The Bridge over the River Dee and the Berwyn Viaduct

As one leaves Llangollen along the A5 towards Corwen, one comes to Berwyn where, almost unnoticed below the road, there is a most complicated system of bridges as the B5103 meets the A5. It is well worth taking a short diversion in order to see this miracle of road and rail engineering

The best place to view this amazing sight is from the other side of the River Dee on the B5103, where there is a good view of the river, the road and the railway all close together below Telford's main A5 road.

The first feature is the Bridge over the River Dee known as the King's Bridge. This bridge is where the B5103 crosses the river, over a series of fine arches, before going under the railway and then rising steeply, in an alarming hairpin bend, to meet the main road. A little further downstream is a fine Chain Bridge, which at the present moment is closed to the public.

The second feature is distinctive Railway Viaduct. This viaduct enables the railway line to climb steeply up above the river from the station in Llangollen, before it disappears into a long tunnel cut into the hills. The viaduct consists of a series of arches, running parallel and just below the main road, one of which acts as a bridge for the B5103 to pass underneath.

The majority of travellers today will pass these feats of road and rail engineering almost unnoticed. However, it is good to stop and look at some of the many engineering features that one can meet along the great road, which Thomas Telford created through North Wales, on its way to Holyhead.

Owain Glyndwr's Mount

Glyndyfrdwy, near Corwen

Photograph
Denbighshire County Council

By kind permission of the Denbighshire County Council

TOUR SIX CONTINUED

WEST OF LLANGOLLEN

Glyndyfrdwy, Owain Glyndwr's Mount & Corwen

Having visited the bridges and the viaduct at Berwyn the tour returns to the A5 and continues westwards towards the village of Glyndyfrdwy, from which Owain Glyndwr derived his name.

About two miles beyond Glyndyfrdwy on the right hand side of the road there is a distinctive mound with Scots Pine trees growing on it. This is **Owain Glyndwr's Mount** and was originally the motte of a former Norman earthwork castle, and later became part of his ancestral home.

According to tradition it was from this mount that Owain Glyndwr was declared Prince of Wales on 16th September 1400. His mansion, destroyed by the English in 1403, was in the field below the mount near the river and the outline of the former moat can still be seen beside the railway line. *NB. The mount and site of the moat are on private land.*

Two miles beyond Owain Glyndwr's Mount and on the B5437 at **Carrog** there is a fine stone bridge over the River Dee built in 1660.

Further evidence of the influence of Owain Glyndwr can be found in the small town of **Corwen,** which was his headquarters and where he gathered his troops before the Battle of Shrewsbury. In the south porch of the church there is an ancient stone, now part of the lintel of the south door, on which there is incised a dagger-like cross, known as Glyndwr's Sword. Tradition states that this cross marks the point of impact of a weapon thrown by Glyndwr, from the hill behind the church, in a fit of anger with the people of Corwen. However, all must have been forgiven, as there is now a modern statue in the Market Square, raised to the memory of Owain Glyndwr, Prince of Wales.

TOUR SIX CONTINUED

WEST OF LLANGOLLEN

Rug Chapel & Visitor Centre

From Corwen the tour continues along the A5 to the junction with the A494 road to Ruthin. Turn right on to the A494 and almost immediately on the left is the CADW entrance to Rug Chapel.

Rug Chapel is a private chapel and was built in 1637 by **Colonel William Salusbury**, a staunch royalist and governor of Denbigh Castle. The lordship of Rug was passed down from the Salusbury family to the **Vaughan** family and then to the **Wynn** family. In 1854 Sir Robert Vaughan restored the exterior of the chapel and added the bell turret.

The interior of Rug Chapel remains much the same today as it did in 1637, and is a rare example of the 'high church' liturgical experiments of Charles I.

The many 17th century fittings include the canopied pews either side of the altar, the altar rails and the sanctuary chair and credence table; the wooden panelling in the nave, the pews and sets of unusual and elaborately carved open benches. At the east-end of the north wall of the nave there is an interesting 17th century wall painting and inscription depicting the transient nature of life and the inevitability of death.

The chief glory of Rug Chapel is its highly decorated and carved roof. Five beams, decorated with a floral design, support the painted roof, which in turn is covered with elaborate national and Christian emblems interspersed with finely carved roof bosses and angels. In the centre of the roof is an unusual painted wooden candelabrum, which has recently been restored.

In the well cared for grounds of the former gamekeeper's cottage CADW, who now manage the property, have created an interesting **Visitor Centre** and exhibition. Just north of Rug, at **Derwen**, there is a fine decorated churchyard cross of the mid to late 15th century, which is also in the care of CADW.

TOUR SIX CONTINUED

WEST OF LLANGOLLEN

A diversion to Llangar Church

Visitors to Llangar Church have to make arrangement to do so with the custodian of Rug Chapel (Tel:01490 412025). From Rug Chapel return to the A5 and then take the B4401 Cynwyd road. Llangar Church is a short distance on the right and down a narrow farm path. NB. Parking is in the lay by on the Cynwyd road.

The isolated church of **All Saints, Llangar**, is set just above the confluence of the River Dee and River Alwen and within a large churchyard filled with a mass of tombstones. The simple whitewashed exterior is a real disguise for its amazing interior, which has been wonderfully restored by CADW after years of neglect. This neglect was because in 1856 a new church was built at Cynwyd, following the rearrangement of the parish boundaries.

As one approaches Llangar Church, through the 18th century lych gate, it soon becomes obvious that the whole church is sloping, due to it being built into the hillside and to the various alterations and additions to original medieval church in the 17th, 18th, and 19th centuries.

The interior of the church is of more interest than the exterior. It has a fine medieval wooden roof with a simple barrelled ‘canopy of honour’ over the altar. On the walls there are several fairly crude wall paintings which were painted as teaching aids to the congregation over the centuries. The two oldest are 14th century and depict a bishop and St Christopher. The huge figure of death on the north wall is dated about 1748.

The furnishings of the church are mostly Georgian and include a fine three-decker pulpit, simple box pews for the gentry and crude benches for villagers. In the gallery, used for a choir and musicians there is an unusual four-sided music stand.

The whole Church of All Saints Llangar makes a wonderful study of rural Welsh church history and architecture.

Rug Chapel

Watercolour by John Ingleby

1794

The National Library of Wales

By kind permission of Llyfrgell Genedlaethol Cymru / The National Library of Wales.

Llangar Church

Watercolour by John Ingleby

1794

The National Library of Wales

Cynwyd Mill. *Lithograph J.Townshend / C.Hullmandel. 1824*

Pont Newydd. *(River Cierw) Aquatint by W.Ellis /E.Pugh 1794.*

THE END OF TOUR SIX

WEST OF LLANGOLLEN

The Waterfalls at Cynwyd & at Pont y Glyn-diffwys

From Llangar Church return to the B4401 and continue on to the Village of Cynwyd. Turn left along a minor road and then take the right fork following the river. The waterfall is behind the cottages, where permission should be sought to park and visit the fall.

Cynwyd Waterfall is at the end of a wooded valley, through which the River Trystion flows rapidly down from the Berwyn Mountains. The river tumbles down the rock face in a series of charming small cascades. In the lithograph of Cynwyd Falls by J.Townshend / C.Hullmandel (1824) he titles the print '*Cunwyd Mill'*. This print clearly depicts a mill and waterwheel at the bottom of the falls, which have now been replaced by a modern house, which sadly rather obscures the view of the fall from the valley.

From Cynwyd waterfall return to Cynwyd and turn right at the B4401 and continue on to the A5. Turn left at the A5 and continue on to Ty-nant and turn left, off the main road, and park the car on what was the original A5 road.

Pont y Glyn-diffwys Waterfall (Pont Newydd) was a favourite subject for 18th and 19th century artists but seems to have been forgotten by present day photographers. This is partly due to the fact it is only marked on the larger scale maps and partly because until recently it was right on the busy main A5 trunk road. This part of the road has now been by-passed and one can have a splendid view of the bridge above the fall 200 yards down the road, from an old recess, set into wall beside Telford's original road. In order to see the fall properly one has to cross Pont y Glyn, standing high over the River Ceirw, and scramble down the side of the valley, where there is an excellent view of the whole fall.

POSTSCRIPT

So I come to the end of my tours of the superb countryside and places of historical interest that surround the ancient town of Llangollen. The combination of this rich variety of scenery confirms my belief that Llangollen makes the ideal centre from which to explore the whole area.

Llangollen itself is a busy town that is full of interest and to the north, south, east and west of it there are historic churches and chapels, castles and houses, as well as beautiful mountains and hills, rivers, valleys and waterfalls.

I hope that any who may come to look at this small short appreciation of Llangollen and its splendid surrounding countryside may also discover for themselves something of the stunning beauty and proud history of this particular part of the Principality of Wales.

2005

BIBLIOGRAPHY

1750	Gentleman's Magazine	January 1750
1750	Views in Wales in Aquatinta	P.Sandby
1812	The Beauties of North Wales	J.Evans
1813	The Principal Rivers of Wales	J.G.Wood
1816	Cambria Depicta	E.Pugh
1817	The Northern Cambrian Mountains	T.Compton
1823	Beauties of Cambria	H.Hughes
1823	Welsh Scenery	Captain Batty
1830	Wales Illustrated	Jones & Co
1835	Wanderings in North Wales	T. Roscoe
1837	The Town & Vale of Llangollen	Simpson's Account
1886	Black's Picturesque Guide to North Wales	
1990	Denbigh, Rhuddlan, Flint, Elwoe Castles	CADW
1990	A Hurried History of Llangollen	G. Sherratt
1993	Rug Chapel & Llanagar Church	CADW
1995	Valle Crucis & Basingwerk Abeys	CADW
1997	A Tour of the Waterfalls of Wales	D.Yerburgh
1999	A Tour of the Abbeys etc of Wales	D.Yerburgh
2000	Powis Castle	The National Trust
2001	Denbighshire People and Places	Dr Charles Kightly
2001	Chirk Castle	The National Trust
2002	Erddig	The National Trust
2002	Borderlands "Castles"	Dr Charles Kightly
2002	Border lands "Sacred Places"	Dr Charles Kightly
2003	Enjoy Medieval Denbighshire	Dr Charles Kightly
2003	Dinas Bran Castle	Dr Charles Kightly
2003	Enjoy Medieval Denbighshire	Dr Charles Kightly
2004	Dolforwyn & Montgomery Castles	CADW
2004	The Ceiriog Valley Walk produced by	The Chirk & Ceiriog Valley Partnership
2004	The Clywedog Valley Trail produced by	The Wrexham County Borough Council
N/D	The History of Ruthin Castle	Reginald de Hereford
N/D	The Guidebook to Plas Newydd & The Ladies of Llangollen	
		Valley Partnership
2004	The Clywedog Valley Trail produced by	The Wrexham County Borough Council
N/D	The History of Ruthin Castle	Reginald de Hereford
N/D	The Guidebook to Plas Newydd & The Ladies of Llangollen	

INDEX

INDEX CONTINUED

ACKNOWLEDGEMENTS

My brother **Peter Yerburgh**, who helped me to put the text on the computer and has come to my rescue on many occasions with amazing patience and skill.

Diana Coleridge, who proof read the text, made many valuable suggestions and took the majority of the photographs that have been reproduced in the book.

Rebecca Kingston, who designed the cover of the book, and then transferred it on to a disk for the printer.

CADW and to the National Trust, for the use of their excellent guide books to the properties that have been included in this book.
Also Cadw Crown Copyright for their kind permission to reproduce the map of the area on page 5 & the photograph on page 8.

The Llangollen Railway Plc for the map of the railway line from Llangollen to Carrog on page 20.

The Denbighshire County Council for permission to reproduce the photograph on page.84.

The images on pages.22, 30, 66, 68, 74, 78, 88, 89 and also the one on the back cover, **by kind permission of Llyfrgell Genedlaethol Cymru / The National Library of Wales.**

Finally the anonymous photographer for the image on page 71, the source of which I have totally failed to track down.

***Front Cover**, Coloured Aquatint, The Vale of Llangollen, Denbighshire.*
Drawn by T.Compton & Engraved by D.Havell. 1816.
***Back Cover**, Copper Engraving, Castell Dinas Bran, Denbighhire.*
Drawn by M.Griffith & Engraved by W. Watts. c.1780.
By kind permission of Llyfrgell Genedlaethol Cymru / The National Library of Wales.